NESARA and The Mark of the Beast

Dr. Scott Young

Copyright © 2020

NESARA and The Mark of the Beast

www.DrScottYoung.com

Publisher Sue Reidel of Logos Publishing

ISBN:
9798685458650

CONTENTS

DEDICATION

I believe that the Bride needs this message the most. They need to know who they are in Christ. He comes for you. But there is work in the Spirit to be done. Your job is to find that work and begin doing it (Luke 12:35). Many of you are concerned with the nature of the 2020 elections and the implications therein. The fascination legislation dubbed NESARA will bring about mighty changes in life. But too many Christians are worried about the practical plan that the Bible will come true with NESARA in the Mark of the Beast. I, therefore, wish to clear up those misunderstandings for you and pray you find peace.

Chapter One

The 2020 Question

If you have made it into 2020, you have felt much like the world is circling the drain. You might even wonder if it's all just a bad dream. You may have lost faith in the words of the people around you on social media, the blather in mainstream media, or the conjuring of those in government. After the global response to the pandemic of 2020 for the COVID 19 virus, we moved right into racial inequality protests and then destructive chaos of criminal rioting. I have also heard some, on Facebook, who jokingly worry about "killer hornets."

There is no one who is not affected by the nature of disruption. When the words of "social distancing, wear your masks, black lives matter, ANTIFA, and racial inequity" create a level of fear, anger and depression in those who hear it on both sides of the ideological fence. For Christians who are supposed to be trusting in the Lord, they also have their own biases around these words based upon their own experiences of their youth. Those experiences create anxieties that they never knew existed. But I contend that God knew that this level of chaos the world is plowing through was known by Him from the moment He opened His mouth to create the foundations of the earth. Some question whether He is hearing; He absolutely is.

But, your response should be inside of the word trust. To whom do you turn when things get out of hand? If your trust is inside the governmental system, it is shaken. If it is inside of your ability to create wealth in your business or investments, then the shutdown of the economies by forces outside of your control pushed you to the brink. If your trust is inside of your family and friend support system, then being shut inside your house with little sports and no new fictional programming on TV incurs levels of unknown depression. When you add news that screams to take away your freedom in exchange for your safety, it might concoct a potion of intense isolation you are unprepared to handle. All of this feels like a prison.

Many Retirement Villas, Assistive Living and Nursing Homes have been hit incredibly hard on two fronts. Firstly, populations over 70 have more of a tendency to be sicker than the rest of their younger neighbors, which initiates responses of those in charge to lockdown the healthy and ill together. See what has happened to Michigan, NYC and other states who put the COVID patients with healthy ones. Many of my patients in Audiology have a strong desire for family interaction during this crisis. But their lack of communication increases the effects of dementia in their cognitive abilities. Staff members, inside of their own fears, respond by feeding the Assistive Living patients under their care three meals a day with plastic forks and no contact by the outside world. This reminds me of another population of whom I serve: the Department of Corrections. These inmates experience isolation due to their crimes. But what crime has the elderly done to deserve this treatment?

All the above must bring the Believer in Christ to the inescapable position of reducing your fear by increasing your trust in the One who made you. The Soul (your Mind, Will and Emotions) are asking great questions in this outrageous timeframe of our lives and is not receiving an answer that makes any sense. There is rampant speculation that Bill Gates, the Gates Foundation and Anthony Fauci are pushing the world to produce a vaccine for COVID 19 to inoculate the populations of the world against this horrible disease.

Since this disease was discovered in Wuhan, China, somewhere in January of 2020, there are questions as to its origin. Did the Chinese Deep State unleash this toxin as an act of terrorism upon the globe to induce this panic shutting down and creating their own level of control over the "sheep" that they call the people?

The CDC is lying to the population. Once told that hundreds of thousands were dying, maybe closer to 9000 were dying directly of this illness. That comes only days after NYC and other disgusting mayors were required to present documentation of why they held the sick with the healthy.

Inside of the vaccines that are presented by the World Health Organizations and the Centers of Disease Control, some believe that a cure might come in 2021 (in reality, vaccines to be safe take six to ten years). That faith in the relief smacks of confidence in the origin of the man-made virus or its properties to not replicate itself into variant forms that are outside of their own containment protocols. The Proposals by the WHO and CDC is to create Contact Tracing with Global Positioning Systems inside of the Apple iPhone software release 13.5.0 developed in May of 2020 to help with those who are diagnosed with the Corona Virus and quarantining the infected from spreading the contagion. If by placing a microchip to facilitate the vaccine that can be read by a scanner at National Football League games by those who enter the stadiums could ensure that groups of people could be safe being together, then the Deep State wishes to promulgate the idea among the masses. But there are varying estimates that as many as 700,000 people will die of the vaccination. Bill Gates understands the risks of the vaccination death rates and is willing to push forward with post-haste for the greater good.

All of that leads the Christian who reads the Bible indicating the following question: could I be getting the Mark of the Beast inside this COVID 19 vaccination coming in 2021? The answer is *Maybe*. But we need to answer a ton of other questions before we can broach the possible solution. I caution the reader to trust in the Word's statements about itself. In John chapter 1, the Disciple makes the fascinating correlation that Jesus intersected with Truth, God and Light all at once. Therefore, the Word of God that is the Bible has the answers for the questions we ask. Let's not allow a YouTube video to supersede the statements of the Bible as we are the Bride of Christ. Let's let God speak for Himself, shall we?

But more importantly related to this discussion is the understanding of money we need to investigate. NESARA, National Economic Stabilization and Recovery Act, will (at the time you are reading this, it may have already fallen into place under a potentially different name) create a new reality for money. It will also require time to disseminate many aspects of its implementation throughout America, while GESARA (global) will be going out to the world. All are asking significant questions relating to the upheaval: What do Money, Vaccines, Diseases and the Mark mean for me?

13

CHAPTER TWO

Definitions of Words

You might feel, as though in this chapter, that I might be taking you to sophomore-level English class where we began to define complex semantics, but we must! Why? If we do not, we risk getting our understandings so far off we can't come back from them. Society struggles on all sides of problems pertaining to the simple point of shared wordings that have multiple meanings to each group. While we don't need to devolve into all those words to understand them, we need to quantify a few of them here.

Doctrine vs. Theology

You might be looking at me sideways when I mention this. Most people think that these two words are synonymous, but they absolutely are not. I hear plenty in the ministry even switch the meanings up.

Doctrine is the way that man defines God. In a broader sense, doctrine can also apply to groups in the shared beliefs that they have in common. Atheists sometimes have their own doctrinal beliefs that include putting down Christians and firm evolutional pursuits. In comparison, *Theology* is the study of the Bible.

One may have an interpretation of the words within the Word, but they need to be in perfect sync with one another for them to be portions of inspired understanding of what God is trying to tell humanity. The Holy Spirit speaks of marriage, business, money, sex, children, cultures and a myriad of other topics, including the definitions of laws. While we may extrapolate those ideas of the laws from the Biblical standpoint and create rules and guidelines, those extrapolations would be in the categories of doctrine.

A perfect example of those two meeting one another comes in the concept of the Trinity. The Trinity was never referred to inside of Scripture, but the word defines the Father, Son and Holy Spirit that they are three pieces of God and all one. Doctrines of use are ideas that explain the nature or the understanding of God. They should NOT replace what the Holy Spirit explains within the Word out of context.

The reason that it is essential to bring these two words into semantics is that I hear the Mark of the Beast brought up in creative and fascinating ways that have little to do with what God intended us to know about the Devil's schemes. John spent time talking about the Mark in Revelation 13 for a reason. On an overall basis, I will indicate *opinion, doctrine or theology* when I write.

Lie and Opinion

Now that we are on the topic of *opinion*, we

need to discuss *lie* and *truth*. Most reason that their own truth is right for them. They wish that others would see it their way so that it would validate their levels of *truth*. I cannot count the number of atheistic professors at universities around America and with whom I have conversed who wish to prove this point more.

Consider this: if you believed that there was no God, why would you need to convince anyone of your ideals? It might be fun to surround yourself with like-minded individuals so that you can share your concepts, but trying to convince another should have no meaning to the Atheist. But too many Atheistic professors believe that it's their solemn duty to rid the young freshman of her strong faith in the God of the Bible. When he has drained the faith out of the kid, he feels vindicated. Don't believe it? I have personally witnessed this occur on college campuses.

But if the Atheist were truly honest with himself, he wouldn't care a whit whether the freshman believed her silliness as he believes. It's all horsepucky to him (as my dad used to say). If the Atheist doctrine is correct, both (the Theist and the Atheist) live eighty years and die to find the hole in the ground desecrating their remains until the sun goes nova and spreads our ashes among the stars. Who really cares? But if the Christian is right, *Whoa Nellie,* the Atheist will be in a world of hurt. Dr. Frank Turek, in his beautiful book "I don't have Enough Faith to Be an Atheist," preaches messages that will explain this train of thought if you wish to further that line of illogic. Check his channel on YouTube called Cross Examined.

Therefore, inside the current culture, one's truth is nothing more than his *opinion.* *Lie* in the Greek is *pseudos*, and if that word seems oddly familiar, it's because we, in English, borrowed most of it to explain our reality. If I used the term pseudo-science, it would be the study of a scientific endeavor that scientists themselves do not believe rises to the level of hard science in which they can quantify. *Lie* means only a partial understanding of *truth.*

Opinion means *gnome* in Greek. It refers to the faculty of reason or judgment and can contain one's purpose for being that can imply one's biases. Does that not sound like the political culture of 2020 before its election? So much bias comes from the Mainstream Media then regurgitated upon the social networks in one form or fashion. A woman may apply her set of reasoning to the application of the choices she might make for herself based upon her judgment of her available facts. On the other hand, another man might respond so differently to the same set of data to move in the complete opposite direction upon how his bias takes him. And then we take that reasoning and judgment to our *opinion* and create our *truths* that seem immutable. But is it an objective *truth?* Do I have to answer that one for you?

The New Testament uses a variety of words for Truth that you can find dotted across the pages. Some of the words for Truth infere that one would be a martyr for speaking it (John 19:37 has a bunch of those words). Specifically, if one gives a testimony but it is found to be false (we call that perjury and it carries a potential felony sentence that can be transmuted without jail time), he would forfeit your life in the false effort. One of my favorite words for truth is *veritas*. This word indicates the need to test your beliefs about a word so that it may be verified. Useful scientific discovery is based upon this conceptualization without bias to the direction the research will lead her. Why don't we employ that word regularly? Our biases attack our reasoning so that our opinions (*Gnome*) are reduced. If research is funded to attach to a particular brand of truth, then the bias is implicit inside of the study.

Satan supports his own positions based on the opposites of God. But Satan is *not* the antithesis of God. Michael, the Archangel, is shown in the book of Revelation. In chapter 20:1-2, we note that at the end of the Tribulation, Satan is bound along with the Anti-Christ, False Prophet, as well as the First Beast inside of the Anti-Christ by none other than this tough guy Michael. Jesus won't need to get his hands dirty. That's why Satan doesn't sit on the other side of the couch from God.

But Satan pulls out his playbook to speak *pseudo* to create his brand of truth. Did you catch that? It's not a full-on lie at all, but his position of truth, which is his opinion. The world falls for this oldest trick in the book to believe that their truth (*Gnome)* is more powerful magic than a truth that is verified as is the Bible. Let's dig into the meat of the book so that we can unmask this enemy of God, shall we?

19

CHAPTER THREE

Tell me more about this Beast?

The number one question is not who the Beast is but who it isn't. "Isn't Biden/Obama/Reagan/Trump the Beast?" But we don't even know what we are asking. I am a classically bad Googler. I somewhat get to what I need, but I almost always need help from my wife or son. I type into the search bar what I believe is what I am saying, but I rarely receive the answer I am seeking.

Why? Because my brain operates differently than most people. That's not always a good thing. I have dyslexia and was informed that it would be hard to make it through high school and to forget about college. But as I trudged through high school doing my best with my learning disability (as well as stuttering disorder and coordination difficulty), I had to work harder than most to accomplish the requisite tasks. It gave me a work ethic that was beyond most average students. My mind processes oppositely than most. I ask the questions that most don't want to ask or ask in the mainstream way, which is why Google and I are not friends.

So, let's apply my own brand of questioning

to the above: *Who is the Beast?* Firstly, you have to know what the Bible *says* about the Beast, because the Word is the genesis of the topic.

Firstly, we must know what the *Mark* means. I don't intend to discuss the modern understanding of the word until later. But there are portions of this phrase we must discuss. The Greek word is *charagma* indicating an etching, stamp or tattoo. It would be an identifier for the person wearing the Mark.

Most who choose a tattoo do with great care. Those choosing a tattoo pick out the concept with which they have an affinity while realizing that it will be on their body for the rest of their lives. Therefore, having the *Mark of the Beast* would be in the same vein as a tattoo. No one would do so without some forethought as to why and where they were pasting an image on their body, especially where Revelation 13:18 depicts "upon the right hand or the forehead."

One idea that might be pertinent to the topic comes from the sporting culture. Teams create logos and quips that are plastered on the chest of a t-shirt or on the forehead of a ball cap. This is known as an identifier that is worn with pride.

The word Beast is *Therion* which signifies a dangerous and venomous animal that cannot be contained. A further study of Scripture is found in Daniel where the author describes four beasts who will come upon the planet wreaking havoc and killing thousands of people in their murderous wake. That conversation of Daniel is innate to the meaning John wrote in the Book of Revelation. So, when we marry the words together into a phrase, the Mark is owned by the Beast.

Think of it this way. Let's say I am an excellent Offensive Coordinator for a successful NFL franchise molding several quarterbacks into Pro Bowlers and championship teams. Your team is rebuilding, suffering through a few horrible seasons and wishes to speak with me about being your Head Coach. Your real desire, actuality, is the revolutionary playbook by which I would employ to develop your team. But you also learn, after investigating me, that I am a cancer in the locker room. I alienate all around me with a constant perfection and just tick them off until they wish to be traded or cut.

How in the world are you going to procure the playbook from my hands without hiring me to your club? The answer is that it won't happen! I am not coming to your city without a contract to be the Head Coach and a fat one to boot.

How could the *Mark* be instituted without the *Beast* in tow? It doesn't happen. Therefore, those who believe that the Mark is going to be etched without your permission before the Beast steps into his new position is not Biblical and not even logical.

The Anti-Christ and the Christ

You might believe that I am moving in reverse order here, but since the Mark of the Beast is the topic of the book, we had to get that out of the way. But let's get a little more fundamental than that.

The Anti-Christ is the object of the question that people are asking. When one asks: who is the Beast, they are asking who the Anti-Christ is. The Anti-Christ is the opposite of Jesus. Christ means *Christos* or *Anointed* in Greek. That's the long-appointed person that would take the Jews out of their lowly position in the world so that they might fulfill their destiny to reign in a world of peace. The Old Testament is replete with references of a Millennial Reign where lions lay beside the lambs and war is conquered.

The Jews did not recognize Jesus when He entered the world on 9/11/3 BC. If you want to know why this fascinating date is Jesus' actual birth, you must investigate *BethlehamStar.net* to find the beautiful answers by a great researcher. Jesus didn't conform to the original concept of being a political leader. He wasn't born to a king in the palace, such as Moses was (Moses was also a type of Christ figure who rescued the Jews from their bondage). But the Jews forgot that Moses rejected his position of political power that he inherited by his adoption inside of the Egyptian pharaohs.

Jesus was born of a virgin, a sin at the time when she was perceived to have had an unnatural extra-marital affair no matter what she had been told by the angel of the Lord. That same angel had to intervene upon Joseph's thoughts so that he wouldn't put Mary out of his house before they had the ceremony of the wedding.

Joseph had descended from a kingly line as Mary had. But that fact was lost to the history because the Jews didn't have control of their destiny under the thumb of Caesar of Rome. Jesus didn't rally the crowds with His oratory skills to whip up sentiment against their oppressors to overthrow the government and take His rightful place as King of kings, of which He could have done. But the First Coming of Christ accomplished the killing of Sin. This released the population of the globe, for *all time,* from the position of death that they were originally sequestered to for eternity. No one was righteous. Therefore, if you don't pay attention as to why Jesus first came, you don't get His Second Coming either.

Jesus predicted in Matthew 24 that there would be false Christs arising in the future. What? It wasn't just ONE false Christ that Jesus intimated at the time when He was answering the Disciple's questions, but many of them. In "The End" by Mark Hitchcock, Dr. Hitchcock pontificated that Satan would have to keep an anti-Christ in his back pocket for every era after Jesus' death to whip him out for the moment he tried to identify (2). What a tiring job for Satan as the liar to humanity? Therefore, if Dr. Hitchcock was correct in his historical assertion about Satan's future boy, Hitler, Mussolini, Mao Si Tung, and Napoleon, to name a few, were groomed for the job that would never come about in their times.

The "War to End All Wars" employed the Kaiser (the leader of the Germans of the time in the 1914-1918 World War One era) who was considered the Anti-Christ of that time. Even President Woodrow Wilson was also considered the Anti-Christ in 1918. He instituted a thirteen point plan to end the war with several conditions including the formation of the League of Nations to resolve conflicts in the future. The League failed as has its sister organization, The United Nations, which holds to the policy to "turn their swords into plow" (Isaiah 2:4). Of course, they have done none of this in either timeframe of their histories.

When will we know the Anti-Christ shows on the globe?

I also hear this question from many people who frequent my classes on End Time topics (called Hope in the Last Days available as a series on DrScottYoung.com): When will the Anti-Christ appear? But they are also innately asking, will I see him in my lifetime?

Many in history have wished to see this dastardly man of sin. Some because he could be connected to worldwide power. Others because he represents the return of Christ in the timeclock of humanity that begins to countdown. I find it fascinating that Christians and End Time teachers alike love to point to a man who may be the Anti-Christ (be he a world leader or a potential world leader). But the Bible clearly indicated that you would not live in the same moment (2 Thessalonians 2:1-11). Let me explain that a little further because of its importance.

"Now concerning the coming of our Lord Jesus Christ and our being gather to Him: We ask you, brothers, not to be easily upset in mind or troubled, either by a spirit or by a message or by a letter as if from us, alleging that the Day of the Lord has come. Don't let anyone deceive you in any way. For that day will not come unless the apostasy comes first and the man of lawlessness is revealed, the son of destruction...(vs. 6) And you know what currently restrains him, so that he will be revealed in his time. For that mystery of lawlessness is already at work, but the one now restraining will do so until he is out of the way, and then the lawlessness one will be revealed...(vs. 9) The coming of the lawless one is based on Satan's working, with all kinds of false miracles, signs and wonders, and with every unrighteous deception among those who are perishing. They perish because they did not accept the love of the truth in order to be saved. For this reason God sends them a strong delusion so that they will believe what is false..."

Let's unpack this slowly. Paul doesn't want the church of Thessalonica to be fooled (and by implication, neither does the Holy Spirit). They need to focus on the truth of the Word. You get fooled when you are inside of your opinion (remember *pseudos*). We are seeing it inside of the times before this Presidential election of 2020 where everyone sees the Anti-Christ or his Mark showing up underneath the bed covers of the enemy.

Verse 3 indicated that the "day will not come unless the apostasy comes first and the man of lawlessness is revealed..." That word has so much controversy in the church that it's not funny. *Apostasia* can be known as a forsaking or defection from truth. Some scholars believe that the church does not invest themselves in the Word of God near the end times, necessitating the Anti-Christ to come on the scene so that she can be tried in her time of Jacob's Trouble. The immense problem with this theory is the blood of Christ. If we needed a time of trouble to "resuscitate" our soul, then we wouldn't *need* the finished work of the Cross. That's a big problem. Others will defend the above time further that the Tribulation comes upon everyone so that their faith can be honed in. It is a somewhat valid point in that the Church may be asleep and needs a wakeup call to get into alignment with God's purposes (think Romans 8:28-29).

The Tribulation, though, is not what most people believe it is going to be. They think it's a terrible time. Matthew 24:24 indicates that if the days were not shortened, no one would make it. A friend of mine, Jeff Swanson Ministries, loves to append that comment by grammatically reorganizing that verse. If you extend it by one day longer, all would be dead. He is dead on the money (sorry about the macabre pun). The seven-year timespan is a horror beyond anything we have ever experienced. There will be wrath as well as choice to follow Jesus in a myriad of paths that would blow your mind if you truly understood it.

Other ministries indicate that the Church is taken away in the *Harpazo* (Rapture) inside of I Thessalonians 4:16-18. Both words have something to do with a "going away." I lean more toward this meaning, but I can answer that in another way that will make sure that the Man of Lawlessness is here only after the Church is gone.

We are the Bride of Christ. Our job is to get married to our Groom. Esther and Ruth hinted that the Jewish ceremony is seven days in duration. There is a multitude of verses that must be fulfilled to accomplish Jesus as the Prince of Peace, fulfilling Himself as the King of kings when He is married to His Bride. All princes remain as such until the abdication or the death of the current king, and the marriage of that prince to his bride. That prince can finally propagate the family for the kingdom to come years down the road.

Whether you believe in a falling away of the Church, which is that we lose our truth (Sword of Christ) that is somewhat true in today's society, or you side with the concept that the Rapture is the removal of the Bride in 2 Thessalonian, both need to have the true Bride out of the way. If elections of America can be swayed effectively toward one candidate when the Church votes in large numbers, consider what the Bride of Christ would do if a man props himself up under the Daniel 9:27 Anti-Christ banner of a peace treaty with Israel.

That's right. He would drown inside the screams of *Anti-Christ* until his voice would be blotted out. It's not the number of the voices that are really at odds with the Anti-Christ, but the ferocity and the fulfillment of the truth from the lips of the Bride that would hold back the tide of Satan. That's how much power you have!

Satan, through his Anti-Christ, cannot step

into his role as the ruler of the earth until the Bride is out of the way. It's the fulfillment of the Bride being the Sea of Glass standing before the King in Revelation 4. John then is bawling his eyes out that no one can open the Seals written by the hand of the Creator until John is told that the Lamb who takes away the sin of the world is worthy of doing so. Jesus then will introduce the Anti-Christ in a future date when we are gone.

CHAPTER FOUR

BEASTS OF THE PAST AND THEIR CHARACTERISTICS

CONQUERORS

Everyone wishes to answer the question I mentioned earlier: "Obama or Trump is the Anti-Christ!" Each time they utter this phraseology, they find that they are wrong, at least at this moment. Since we have explained that the Church is out of the way, you need to answer the obvious...why? At the second the Anti-Christ enters the scene for humanity, the Church would know it. He would be paralyzed by his agenda being known. It was written in a two-thousand-year-old book. (In actuality, it is around 6000 years for all the books, but who's counting.)

Let's talk about the characteristics of the man that will embody the level of evil never heard before. I know that most believe that this man of Lawlessness, as II Thessalonians indicates, will be only a little worse than Hitler. But how could he be worse than Hitler? Each time the Beast inserts himself upon the planet, we see that millions of people die. I would heartily disagree that Hitler was only a small step down from the future Anti-Christ. But what I *would* agree was that Joseph Stalin, Adolph Hitler, and Napoleon Bonaparte were also types of Anti-Christ, which fulfills Matthew 24's intimation that there would be many Anti-Christ figures.

Inside of Revelation 6:2, Jesus will introduce the Anti-Christ as a man who rides on a white horse and has a bow with no arrows but moves out to be a conquering victor. Some pontificates divine that John is referring to Jesus in and of Himself, but that makes absolutely no sense.

Jesus has arrows meaning that He has the power to accomplish whatever He wishes to. Jesus also has the ability to conquer but doesn't need to ride a white horse without arrows to do so. Jesus will come back on a white horse in Revelation 17:14 with His "Called, Chosen and Faithful" to completely destroy His enemies. (If you wish to know more, you can go to my website to see more info through videos and other media to understand what John was indicating.) That only comes at the end of the Tribulation. But this man is none of the above.

Also, Jesus wouldn't open the First Seal (the first of the judgments listed in Revelation that reveals Himself on the planet) to reveal Himself as a conqueror. Nope, this is the Anti-Christ. He is therefore imbued with the First Beast (Revelation 13), who creates a world of hurt for the earth. The Anti-Christ already has a Body, Soul and Spirit; but when the First Seal is cracked open by Jesus, the Tribulation is open for business. That opening only begins at the Daniel 9:27 signing of the peace treaty with many nations to have a peace in Israel that will last for only half of the seven-year period. The Anti-Christ will break that peace initiative.

We then realize that the Anti-Christ would have to be a great orator with supernatural power to bring people and nations together that is similar to the men of the past who dominated the world in their own image. Adolph Hitler preached peace for his country as he took power, through underhanded means called *The Night of Long Nights* in 1934. Hitler killed all his political opponents after he was catapulted into his leadership as chancellor of Germany during the worldwide depression. His means were nefarious only to his political opponents, whereas the masses watched him create a peace and prosperity they hadn't experienced since the end of World War One.

In Russia, the Czars ruled for generations. They kept the people in roles of semi-slavery just above eking out their own subsistence. Vladimir Lenin pushed upon the scene in 1917 as a popular orator promulgating the role of the people above the rulers who benefited from them. The peasant uprising interrupted the First War from their participation so that they could sustain their own revolution of ideas that lasted until 1922. Lenin would not see his empire of Communism grow into the powerhouse it would become under Joseph Stalin.

Hitler was directly responsible for the European war that took more than 40 million, as well as eleven million he ordered to die in the Final Solution (six million Jews and five million other undesirables). Stalin, pushing the goals of the Communist Party and reorganizing the government under the Marxist ideals of a working people, distrusted his own loyalists enough to wipe out his government twice in his reign and killing off untold millions ranging from 20-30 million Russians. They wouldn't cower to his ultimate demands of complete servitude to the state. So, the Anti-Christ is a brutal conqueror. Got it. But what else?

Once you understand that the Beast has to be in place (we will talk more about his beginning in a bit), most will ask the next obvious question that is deeply embedded in their minds: what does the Mark entail?

The Mark, in centuries past, was not considered heavily. It was thought by some to be a tattoo. I began reading end-time novels but mostly non-fiction. Anything I could get my fingers on the topic, I would devour. In the 70-80s, we used to believe that the Mark of the Beast was a bar code that is used to identify packages and consumer items alike. We were terrified that someone might plant their signifier upon us, and we would not be able to come back to the Lord; it would be considered the unpardonable sin.

In the 1990s to early 2000s, we juxtaposed our worry on the chips that were implanted in the credit cards we carry today. But did you know that in 2016, all businesses had to ditch their current credit card processing machines that didn't have the chip readers for the more modern update of which all are used to when purchasing anything at convenient stores?

Those chips have a tremendous capacity to carry all of one's data inside of the memory that may include medical files, financial files and GPS coordinates to the person if they were kidnapped or harmed in a criminal case.

Where the Chip Dips

These microprocessors are in our future in one way or the other. The gigabit limits are not a problem for the mounds of data we might wish to load upon them. Smartphones of the era already are conditioning people to accept geo-tagging themselves so that their family and friends can find them along with their music, financial data and passwords, to name a few apps. The concept of inserting a biomedical chip in the right hand won't be much of a logical leap to those who don't understand what the Bible states about it.

I believe that the Church/Bride will be in Heaven getting married to the Lamb (much can be written about that, and I have done so in my other books). Without us on the planet, there will be a significant lack of information that Matthew 24 indicated will exist at the beginning of the End Times. The *severe deception* spoken of leads the reader to understand that the mind-numbing information for those left upon the world will not have enough veritas to grapple with the overload of clever stories created to sidestep one's logic. It will make sense to have this chip readily given and accepted by the massive majority of the population.

Since we already have accepted technology

in our pockets and on our wrists, humanity will integrate this new usage of invasion of one's privacy in means that normally come: a loss of freedom always is transferred for greater security in those who feel their life or livelihood's threatened.

A lithium-based rechargeable battery is already available to the planet that would not need an external power source with the nature of the heat generated by the body. If it could be placed within the body safely, people will adopt the technology.

Possible Deceptions for the Mark Integration

One of the mechanisms I believe might have a strong possibility for the need for the Mark of the Beast during the middle of the Tribulation (of which we will cover the WHEN later in the book), would be related to a potential fraud case. Let me depict for you what I mean.

You are a person of faith that has come to Christ after the beginning of the Tribulation when your wife has left the planet in the world-wide Rapture of the Church. You didn't get it at the time but now have figured out the truth behind her disappearance. It's been a long road of discovery of your sin, life and circumstances within the global disturbances that come fast and furious.

You have been listening to the 144,000 Saints who are young Jewish men who have committed themselves to God right after the Bride of Christ left, realizing that they were wrong about their faith and turned to Jesus. They display incredible insight that adjusted your mind to Christ the moment that one of them spoke in your town.

Now, you are spinning. The Anti-Christ has traveled to Jerusalem just last week and has set himself up in the Temple, driving out the religious Jews in the act of brazen ugliness the likes of which you haven't seen in the worst porno film in the days of your youth. There were human sacrifices that were glorified by the Mainstream Media that disgusts you until you flick the video stream off.

As you traverse to work, your phone buzzes with an Emergency Broadcast tone reminiscent in the years you have heard it time and again announcing something terrible was about to occur. This time, it's personal. The authorities that you don't trust to take out your garbage indicate that you should check your personal credit score. You flash on it as you pull your car over to the side of the road delaying your travel to work.

A credit score of 758 with no significant debt other than your house pops up with red marks everywhere. Someone has hacked your credit and tanked the score to 350 and steadily dropping. More than a million dollars of loans ranging from car loans, credit card debt, personal guaranteed loans and two new houses show up on the reports in other cities you have never visited. You have no idea how you will untangle yourself from this mess. You believe that you will be fired if your credit is this low, while bankruptcy and foreclosure seem to be knocking upon the door of your heart.

Sound like a crazy scenario? Maybe! But consider what it takes to get people to choose for themselves. They need a crisis too many times to move to the less desirous options available. This would be one possible scenario in which Anti-Christ's government would push out a massive fraud to the people of the world to get them to sign up for the Mark that would wipe out that point of fraud. Those that don't sign up? Well, they will be hunted from a financial mechanism because they may have been the exact people who propagated those crimes.

Fear is a powerful motivator to create a spot in which those give over their rights to the governments of the world so that safety or security can be attained. Could it also be a pervasive pandemic with a higher mortality rate than the fake one for COVID 19? Sure. But all of those would lead to the same point. You are glad to take the Mark and bow to the one who saved you.

Buy and Sell

Most prophecy teachers spend significant energy investing in the buying of goods by the world, while few ever converse about the torrent of emotional states for those who are in the position of selling products and services. As a business owner and if I happened to live in that time of the Mark, I would be faced with the complete closure of my business, wrecking my ability to pay my employees, family, creditors, and loss of any income. The Mark mandates of the future would undoubtedly be imposed upon the businesses first. Some companies that are large in size might have already caved by the time that the general citizen had a whiff of the chaos to come.

The small and medium-sized organizations of all types would close almost immediately as their non-compliance would lead to the most significant unemployment crunch in the history of the world. With unemployment upwards of 40%, an all-encompassing depression of gigantic proportions would be thrust upon the people of the world. It might happen just because millions were missing from the planet in the Rapture of the Bride.

Along with unemployment of Biblical proportions, the economies would topple around the world, leading to suicide, black markets for goods and wanton killings that make so little sense as mental disorders overwhelm the facilities of the people. Then one would not be able to find the basics of life, let allow the technologies of which we rely on, to sustain the standards to which most are accustomed. All people would notice that their lot was downgraded drastically to include more misery than they had known because there are suddenly no stores to purchase. The owners of those stores cannot find stock for their shelves, and the colossal depression of the world deepens. But we need to understand the level of cash flow concerning the Mark of the Beast, so we must therefore discuss the origins of the monetary system.

39

NESARA and The Mark of the Beast

CHAPTER FIVE

The Flow of Cash – The Federal Reserve

One facet of what we are seeing in the third quarter of 2020 is a loss of control by the Elite. Donald J. Trump is one of the few billionaires who is not swayed by the oligarchy of the left-leaning Cabal who wishes to rip apart the world for its own aims. Each time a person becomes successful enough, there tends to be a powerbroker either in the wings to guide that individual or another who propels that person into the nature of power.

But world power doesn't come without the cash. That's why it's so fascinating that Mr. Trump has completed his rise to power firstly through his business dealings. He is the first man to ascend to that office, other than prominent George Washington. Of course, he had money. But why would he take that kind of headache on? He has been rejected by those who called him their friends throughout the years he rumbled with the cool crowds of America.

The simple reason is that he has taken on the Cabal because he saw them for what they are: evil. The Cabal has set up the cash system called the Federal Reserve back in 1913.

What's interesting about the creation of the Federal Reserve by many American Central Bankers was that Isa Strauss, Benjamin Guggenheim and John Jacob Astor, III all were on a fateful voyage from America on the newly built Titanic in April of 1912.   J.P. Morgan funded and built the Titanic but deleted his ticket upon its maiden sailing right before it left the English docks.   The three above men were tycoons and would be considered billionaires of our time. Surprisingly, all three perished on the iceberg that killed most of the crew and passengers.   Let me ask you?   Can you remember the last time wealthy and powerful men chose to die on a ship when they could have finagled their way off the boat?   That's right, neither can I!   But that's not the unique part of the story.   They were all vehemently against the creation of the third iteration of the Central Bank in America, and the Federal Reserve that would be instituted on December 23, 1913, by Woodrow Wilson, who regretted it for the rest of his life by his memoirs (1).

The powerbrokers of the time took their competition out on the sinking of the unsinkable.   Once the Federal Reserve, which has nothing to do with the Government of the United States whatsoever, came to power, nothing was stopping it from wreaking havoc upon the economies of the world. Only one year later, in 1914, the most auspicious beginning of a conflict occurred by killing Archduke Ferdinand and his wife, which blew up into a conflict called the *War to End All Wars*. Thirty million people about the globe ending on

November 11, 1918, at eleven AM. Did you know that they fired their shells at one another even though the treaty was signed to cease hostilities up until that morning? But Power Brokers made millions into billions for America that created the Roaring 20s.

The Great Depression of the 30s was initiated by the same Cabal of the Central Bankers of the Federal Reserve. These bankers created a system in which an individual shareholder only had to place 10% down to purchase a stock, then had the rug pulled out from underneath him in October 1929. This established the seeds of the bank failures and land grabs of the filthy wealthy. The country would pay for its reliance upon the dollar that was weakening each day.

The Internal Revenue Service (IRS) took the salaries of the people (taxation without fair representation) and paid it back to the Federal Reserve's debts that the nation owed to the banks who then created the money that was earned by the sweat of their labor. I know that last sentence is a mouthful, but you might want to sit back and chew on that a little while longer. I have this information based upon a huge amount of research, as well as inside information from those who have worked for the IRS. It's the greatest transfer of wealth in the history of man, and the rest of the earth worked along the same evil scheme to kill off the working men and women of the world in their debts.

In 1933, Franklin Delano Roosevelt (FDR) required the gold returned to the government to pay for the mounting debts they owed to the Federal Reserve. FDR gave each person holding gold the current value of $20.60 per ounce. But in 1934, the value had increased artificially to over $33 an ounce (3). Therefore, all our money was instantly devalued, while the Feds had their cash and required more from every citizen daily.

But, when Trump took office, he vowed to reverse the Feds hold on America by declaring, firstly under the table through the Q movement, that he would return America, and thus the world, upon a precious metals standard, namely gold. How do you do that?

Well, you might already know this, but essentially to bankrupt the Federal Reserve through the CARES act #2 that enacted the Payroll Protection Program (PPP) that popped up for businesses in March of 2020. Trump placed the Fed under the Treasury Department and required them to give money to millions of small businesses on average for these small businesses of $59K per company. All of it had a proviso act that it was granted or forgiven from repayment if the company used it primarily for payroll. That's when I started putting these puzzle pieces together with the research I did on the Federal Reserve for years.

More Background of the Fed along with the War that is Playing out in 2020

Ok now, at this point, you might feel like you dropped into a famous movie called "The Matrix." In this 1999 film, there is a powerful scene of awakening. Many Christians have noted that "The Matrix" is a type of analogy of the Believer's walk out of darkness and into the light. Neo is a talented computer programmer for a large firm in New York City but has an alternate life in the underground of hacking software for personal gain. This fascinating dichotomy leads him to people who may be affecting the system of governance in the world, creating a disturbance in the balance of the world in which he also feels the imbalance. He comes across references to Morpheus and Trinity, which are known as mythical characters he believes are real who have hacked the political and economic system in unknown ways to Neo.

Once the beautiful Trinity prompts him to search deeper into his alternate reality, she introduces him to the infamous Morpheus after Neo has been captured by supposedly Deep State operatives in the government who wish to get their arch-nemeses, Trinity and Morpheus. Morpheus promises to bring Neo up to speed, but the young man must make a choice: Blue Pill allows him to back out of his fantasy life and believe whatever he wishes about his encounter versus the Red Pill brings him deeper into the Rabbit Hole (in *Alice and Wonderland* fashion) to know what the Matrix is. This awakening is common in those who have understood what the government agencies have been feeding Americans to believe the mainstream narrative. But let's follow that Red Pill a little farther, shall we? You need to know why these points of the Federal Reserve are so nefarious in their pursuit of underground Deep State activities that lead you so far astray.

NESARA Background

Farmers in the 1970s were sick of the government taking their land and dictating the crops they could plant. They chose to hire a collective attorney to look at the Constitutional evidence for this precedent and found one under the 14th Amendment in Section four: "The Validity of the public debt of the United States, authorized by law, including debts incurred for payment of pensions and bounties for services in suppressing insurrection or rebellion, shall not be questioned. But neither the United States nor any State shall assume or pay any debt or obligation incurred in aid of insurrection or rebellion against the United States, or any claim for the loss or emancipation of any slave; but all such debts, obligations and claims shall be held illegal and void (4)."

Basically, what the Amendment states is that one cannot be liable for a debt that came from a group who was outside of the Constitution to create a rebellion against its citizens. It's a fascinating but complicated law that indicated how foreign interests that subvert our nation were creating a criminal liability to be paid back to those entities. One should and does pay back legal debts owed, but those with which were made inside of the illegal Federal Reserve that we have already shown is owned by foreign powers, including the British Crown, were not legal. Those types of contracts where both parties do not understand what kind of loan or payments are due to whom and how can be shown as null and void based upon Constitutional law.

The NESARA ruling found a way that all of the debts created by the Federal Reserve through the large banks for mortgage loans, car loans, credit cards and other capricious debts of that created a level of illegality in which the borrower should be notified as to the nature of the loan. I remember in 2003, before the housing crisis of 2008, that a mortgage broker in Denver was attempting to get Wendy and me to choose a Three to Five Year ARM for our loan. It would essentially reduce our payments from the typical loan from $3000 a month to less than $1200, allowing us only to pay the interest, while the value of the house rose enough to refinance the loan with a new home with the increased rate of value.

Something was filtering through both of our spirits at the time to say, "Heck no dude!" That exact type of loan, when the three to five-year term came due, was the reason for the housing crisis and the forfeiture of the houses by people who could never afford their current home with the conventional mortgage payment who believed the lie from the broker. The banks received the house back and were able to resell it without having to pay the homeowner any of the assets they had built up in the payment process. This is precisely what happened to the farmers in various ways, and I am so glad for this find by the farmers.

There is a group that I refer to as the Anti-

Cabalists who have tried to bring freedom in America for many years, even during that 2008 crisis. They have long tired of the evil Cabal of the world's central banks and Federal Reserve pedophiles who have literally raped our children in their Satanic gain along with the stealing of our money. The World Settlement Fund was created with gold in the Philippines (the gold was discovered, in part, by America during World War Two) and in China of $47 Trillion in backed currency. It was to release 140 countries of their debts to the Cabal and the Central Banks who have enslaved them by the illegal means of collateral debt along with fractional banking loans designed to take the interest upfront without the borrower being able to pay the principal back in a sufficient timeframe. These funds were blocked from being enacted by the Corporation of Washington DC (that's right folks, the District of Columbia has been a recognized corporation to oust themselves from the Constitutional laws of our land) to delete the penalties of enacting the debt enslavement. The Anti-Cabalists have been fighting for years with a lien against the Fed from the 2011 transfer of funds that the Fed stole to free these countries.

The Global Collateral Account had $93 Quadrillion in asset-backed funds. They were to to release the rest of the debt system from the fiat currency the Fed creates to pay themselves. That debt Americans incur also fuels an incalculable interest off of the sweat of your labor inside the unconstitutional IRS taxation of income. Barack Obama would not allow any of these funds, along with George Bush Junior and his father, who was a shadow president during his son's term, by telling The Hague World Court that Obama would not sign off of the fund's release in July of 2011.

NESARA was supposed to be released in 2000 before the Global Collateral Account monies were blocked from American presidents' Bush junior and senior destroyed Building Seven in the World Trade Center. Building Seven of the World Trade Center should be known as the worst coverup in American history by Larry Silverstein (who took out a several Trillion backed insurance policy against the building only weeks before 9/11). The BBC reported, on the morning of September 11, 2001, that his building was too fire damaged to sustain its weight and that it needed to be pulled. The building came down in seven seconds, defying the laws of physics. Many architects and engineers who understand of the nature of the collapse of a building know that without weeks of planning, with demolitions placed at the right spots, the building will not be an effective "pull" (which was exactly what occurred on 9/11 by any video evidence you can readily search for).

NESARA'S Funding and Release of Debts

Right now, you feel a little like you are tumbling down that proverbial rabbit hole. The evidence seems too far out there to be true. I am trying to lead you to the research, but many won't believe it or maybe wouldn't be able to find it due to social media or website removals of this evidence that I have accumulated along with others for more than ten years.

These Cabalists, including George Soros, JP Morgan Trusts, Rockefeller families, the British Crown, Bill and Hillary Clinton, the Bush Families and many others, have wished to keep the funds from the world to enslave the people. In 2020, when Donald Trump placed the Fed underneath the Treasury, as I mentioned above, he required the Fed to take on debt from companies struggling through the fake proliferation of the Corona Virus. The President was defunding them at an alarming rate for economists who relied on the reliability of the Fed for money flow, and reduction of debt in our economy. The balance between deflation and inflation has been so endemic in our economic makeup that we have come to believe in its power to control the Capital of the world.

Nothing could be farther than the truth. When one wishes to declare bankruptcy, it's a common practice for the borrower to purchase on his credit cards to the maximum items which cannot be repossessed by the court system to hide those assets before he becomes financially unstable. That's exactly what Trump has done with the defunding of the Cabal. He made them pay for all his initiatives to give money back to the people before he drops them into the ocean of their own puke filled fiat currency.

Debts will be released from car loans, credit cards and house payments at an alarming rate for the Central Banks because they cannot accommodate that non-payment without abject failure of their balance sheets since they have loaned out more than they have in their coffers. And since the Fiat Currency is only backed by the ability of the Fed to lie to the public as does any Central Bank throughout history, their responses to their creditors will fold like a house of cards.

But Trump won't allow you to be swindled again as when the banks failed in 1929 where no one could receive the cash they held in the private banks. If you have $1000 in savings, you will still have $1000 in savings; but the Gold Backed Standard of currency, which might be called Rainbow Currency or some other adjusted name, won't have the Central Banks stealing from you with the IRS income tax which pays its cash to the Feds through the Treasury for more than a century of fraud. That's why this transition is and will be so crucial to the world. We will now turn to the meaning of the Currency transition and the Mark.

CHAPTER SIX

What does NESARA mean for me?

What does this all mean? Trump stepped the people of America, and in essence, the world, from the Fiat monetary system (money created from nothing other than the backing of the Fed) into a Gold-Backed Quantum Financial System (QFS). The President worked to revalue the currency of those people in the world who weren't raping and pillaging through the banking systems that were fraudulent in and of themselves. I didn't use that term, raping haphazardly, since Adrenochrome and the killing of children inside of their evil schemes are related to those who have stolen from the people of the world inside of the banks. But how would we ever get back to the point of the control that money has for those who wish to rule the world?

We would firstly find that the Christians will have to be missing from the planet so that those who scheme against humanity can take control of it all over again through a digital platform that the Anti-Cabalists have created their aforementioned Rainbow Currency. But God has a plan for the world before He has a plan for the Tribulation to occur.

God, through His personality called Holy Spirit, is allowing a level of freedom. His character of Liberty is flowing through the world so that He can find His Faithful Bride *doing* the work (Luke 12:35-37) that they were called to accomplish BEFORE Jesus takes her away to the Bridal Suite and the Wedding Feast of the future.

"Be ready for service and have your lamps lit. You must be like people waiting for their master to return from the wedding banquet so that when He comes and knocks, they can open the door for Him at once. Those slaves the master will find alert when He comes will be blessed. I assure you: He will get read, have them recline at the table, the come and serve them (Luke 12:35-37)." There are so many groups of people inside of this passage that I wrote a whole book on the topic (DrScottYoung.com). But suffice it to say, you are the Faithful that must be ready for service with your lamps lit (meaning that the Holy Spirit is inside of you with the Word of God flowing in your life,) so that He can take you for the Wedding of the Lamb in Heaven.

Now, once the Rapture of the Bride occurs, the conqueror of Revelation 6 that Jesus will introduce, can create a process by which he may control the world since the Revaluation of Currency must include the world inside of NESARA and GESARA. Both the world and America must have a role in the same financial currency response to one another. People also ask all the time: Isn't that the Mark of the Beast in which you cannot buy and sell without this Mark? Nope!

Why? Because NESARA is based inside of freedom and debt forgiveness. The Cabal would never approve of debt forgiveness and freedom. They want Communism, Socialism (now stupidly called Democratic Socialism by Bernie Sanders) and Totalitarianism. Socialism and the Fiat currency require the individual to comply and not grow outside of the governmental controls put in place, and all funds are in the possession of the government. When a totalitarian government has control, individuals of the state are property therein and have no freedoms while they are in debt to their eyeballs.

Therefore, the Anti-Christ to come must replace, or frankly may bastardize, the national currencies so that they come in line with a global currency. What President Trump is creating is a national currency allowing for each country to back her financial system upon a precious metal/stone finite amount of money that keeps the standard of the money in high value. They need the shift back to a worthless currency.

Shifting Currencies

It's super easy for Christians who don't spend much time in the Word to feel that the shift happening in 2020 and 2021 toward the NESARA Gold-Backed Currency is either a new era of peace for one thousand years or the initialization of the Mark of the Beast. It's neither.

Over the centuries in America and in Europe, Central Bankers have striven to impale their concept of currency and profit off the people. At times, those currencies took hold due to cataclysmic events, mostly known as run on the banks. People were scared that their money wasn't good anymore in their market dealings and required the bank to stop holding it for the people. Once the run began, the banks would go belly up and funds run dry for business ventures. Central Banks then swooped in to hogtie the masses until they were sidled with a financial debt burden from their own money and the speculation that the Central Banks make on that money to crush the will of the people. When, in the future, the people desire to throw off their oppressors, then a revolution begins.

The Revolutionary War had something to do with this type of currency shifting where the British Crown wished to profit off the sweat off of the people's backs in their colonies without representation of where the money was being used. King George III did just that. The war wasn't about people doing something wrong, but them wanting to choose the path in which their money was proffered. Thomas Jefferson hated the idea of Central Banks and pushed heartily throughout his life to keep the dogs at bay.

Therefore, even when Trump shifts our economic reasoning over into a Gold-Backed Standard of Currency, it will last only for a time. People will believe the lie that they could be better off or could use less tyranny than they are experiencing. A war tends to do the trick.

Ezekiel 38-39 War

Ezekiel spent considerable time describing a war that has perplexed Biblical Scholars for years. While I don't want to explain all the features of the war, I will give a few details. (You can see my whole YouTube series which is the Third called *Hope in the Last Days* called *Ezekiel's War.*)

Firstly, Russia and its general called Gog begin a campaign of jealousy over Israel's riches and stirs up a cavalcade of disgruntled nations around the Middle East, Southern Europe and Northern Africa. They are all at this time Muslim and create a vast army to come and get busy against the Jews. The world suddenly notices that these armies come down in a rush to kill the Jews. It's one of the more fascinating references in Ezekiel 38 where he notes that a people could reckon what an army's intention without being there, which could only occur with current satellite technology and people groups such as the United Nations divining their goals to horde up treasures in Israel.

When the armies stop in the eastern mountains from Jerusalem, three things start to occur: 1. An earthquake localized to those mountains (Ez. 38:19-20); 2. A weapon that creates confusion in its own military (vs.21); and 3) the armies fighting against themselves (vs. 22) until Israel cleans up. Israel spends seven months burying the dead and seven years picking up the weapons for their usages.

During these passages, God, through Ezekiel's unique voice, indicated so many points that could not have occurred until modern times. One was that the peoples of the earth would know the intentions of the invading armies of Gog. In ancient times, the king would send his general to a faraway country with his signate rings and specificities of orders about what to accomplish, trusting that that leader would follow the commands. There was a faith that the man would do as the monarch ordered, but no evidence of the details until the campaign had ended and the king was given the report of the defeat or conquest. But in Ezekiel's account in chapter 38, the other nations of the planet realize that they have come to loot Israel for her great wealth. How??? I believe it's due to satellite imagery and cell phone communication. That's why this is a future prophecy. There are also references of air to air and ground to air missiles in chapter 39. Fascinating.

But why does that matter? After Israel wins and with the supposed knowledge to the world that the Lord of the Universe who will indicate to the people of the world that it was by His doing, the Jews go on their own offensive. Chapter 39 clarifies that the offending nations will have their port cities (most probably Russian cities somewhere in those towns by the sea) suffer a fiery wrath for their transgressions of Israel, and the plans of God for her protection. Here we have another foreword thinking weapon of destruction that could not occur in any ancient time until the 20th century. Israel has always been known to bring retaliation upon her enemies *after* she has been transgressed against.

With this backdrop, I can now potentially insert the postulates that Israel will be a fully unwalled city and have great wealth.

One of the more curious passages that have

made ALL prophecy teachers stumble is the reference: "After a long time, you will be summoned. In the last years, you will enter a land that has been restored from war and regathered from many peoples to the mountains of Israel, which had long been a ruin. They brought out from the peoples, and all of them now live securely (Ezekiel 38:8, HCSB)." Let's detail this passage a bit.

God intimated that they would be separated from the native land. This positively occurred in 70 AD where they were utterly dispersed from their ancient rite of the land by the mountains. In 1948, President Harry S. Truman recognized the people of Israel as a conglomerate people with which the Muslims would never agree. Their land was restored by the wars of the Crusades and other desolations of the crops of the peoples who lived for almost 1900 years, whereas the genetic Israelites who come back brought significant property by agricultural and economical means to this tiny plot of land.

The last portion of the verse uses a puzzling phrase called *Betah* in Hebrew, which means to live without a care or confidence and hope. This all occurs *before* God kicks the rear of the enemy who will invade their soil. Some have postulated that since not all of Israel is walled up that that purports the concept of security. I wondered about that for such a long time. But what if we are wrong?

What if God has a switchover of currency, the GESARA, for the world in which all wars are outlawed (something that Trump and the Anti-Cabalists intimate inside of the conditions of

GESARA living war-free with your neighbors), but these nations don't feel the same equality over time? Just because you have a Gold (or precious jewel) backed currency doesn't mean that all will have the equality of Communism! No, there will still be a creation of equity for the work one creates. If you work hard, you have the potential to make a great living, as happens in the freer nations today without NESARA/GESARA, but it doesn't delete the mentality that I can steal the lands or treasures by my own greed. If you noted that someone else has more than you, your own sin nature might come to play, as it does today, to motivate criminal behavior.

That is one of the possible reasons for the Ezekiel 38-39 War that comes along to devastate the invading nations. It is possible that the armies covering the Middle East toward Israel are jealous of the amount of wealth that the Jews will create. The aim of Gog and his cohorts is nothing more than the destruction and thievery of the wealthy people of Israel. In this case, I can easily see how the GESARA principle of a Gold-Backed currency, through reducing the need of war to acquire what you wish, would lead to selfishness by opposing philosophies illegally obtaining valuables.

But once this incredibly short war (possibly within a week or two in the way that the Scripture describes) is completed, there will be a need for a peace treaty. Treaties only are required by the winning parties with the losers to ensure a potential cessation of hostilities for the future. But consider that Ezekiel noted that the nations against the Jews aren't devastated themselves. They are just militarily humbled and would need to sue for peace. Since no one has ever been able to successfully create a peace treaty with Israel and the entirety of the world, then the seeds of the introduction of the Anti-Christ's rise to power is set in place. Let's investigate how he arises from the Biblical landscape.

CHAPTER SEVEN

THE RISE OF THE ANTI-CHRIST

One of the most asked questions on my YouTube channel and in my classes is the potential identity and introduction of the Anti-Christ. Scripture is relatively clear on this topic, but it does take bouncing about the books of the Old and New Testament to find them: "It is the glory of God to conceal a matter, and the glory of kings to investigate a matter (Proverbs 25:2, HCSB)." I believe that that is one of my life's missions for the body of Christ. I am one of those people who investigate (*Haqar* – search out, examine thoroughly) matters about which people ask.

Everyone wants to know who this character is. People regularly point to a known political figure, as I mentioned in the first chapter. I also referred that the Bride would not know the person of the Anti-Christ until she is removed by her husband, Jesus. But we can discern quite a bit about him.

Scripture indicates that he will be a man of Lawlessness (II Thess. 2:2) and that he will be arrogant. Daniel 7:8 illustrates that the Anti-Christ will be of many nations who rise and has a mouth of arrogance. In Hebrew, *Rab*, means that he will be a great and powerful master. The word refers to arrogance but also can be one who commands and knows that others will follow. But one of the largest prognosticators is revealed in Daniel 9:27: "He will make a firm covenant with many for one week, but in the middle of the week he will put a stop to sacrifices and offering. And the abomination of desolation will be on a wing of the temple until the decreed destruction is poured out on the desolator." Let's detail each portion of this out.

Firm Covenant for One Week

I wish ole' Danny here would say seven years to make it easy, but the Lord doesn't speak in the simplest terms at times, especially of the future. A *Firm Covenant* contains the meaning of a constitution or alliance of people, which doesn't come out of existence unless there is conflict preceding it. This treaty, as some versions also utilize, allows for a one week timeframe. This is a direct reference to a seven-year period of time.

Daniel spoke in many riddles that are difficult to separate for most readers. I also struggle with his writings to this day. He even later started to scribe another of the angel's messages and was told to seal that conversation up until the end times. This mirrors what John, in the Book of Revelation, tries to unveil when the angels warn of the same communication to those who would read his words. Obviously, it was too time or specific, because no one should ever know their future. Knowing that information can lead to horrible breaches of belief relating to the journey. If you knew you would live for ten years, would you be reckless in your pursuit of happiness? Probably.

The Anti-Christ, whom this passage bespoke, will negotiate a peace treaty with many nations for Israel for seven years so that no one can break it easily. It gives the Jews a strength and confidence that they have been the winner of the written agreement. The Anti-Christ will broker a covenant that no one in the history of the world will ever touch. That includes Donald Trump, who negotiated a peace accord with Israel and the United Arab Emirates in August of 2020. That had nothing to do with the nature of a set period of time, which means that it cannot be this peace treaty no matter what you hear.

Middle of the Week Sacrifices End

Here is an excellent example of how God communicates with His people. He does not tell us the *Whens* and the *Hows*, but He does indicate the *Who* and the *Whys*. I promulgate this point throughout my teaching in *The Hope in the Last Days* series. Don't try to answer what God doesn't say. You will always be wrong. For example, I decided to move my office at the prompting of the Lord in April of 2020. I didn't tell anyone other than my co-owner Cathleen. The rest of them didn't need to know until the time was closer. They needed to focus on their own business at hand. Without being condescending here, I was operating in the same nature of God who only tells us when He wishes us to know. Therefore, God tells us in the middle of the week, the Anti-Christ will revert in nature of being a peaceful leader to a warring one. Revelation 13 also gives much of this path that we will detail, which explains the progression of the Anti-Christ to his domination of those within the planet.

Suffice it to say that the Anti-Christ will have a change of heart to stop what the Jews feel is most important: their Temple. We know *that* there *will* be a Temple, and *that* it will at least one round of Sacrifices yearly (meaning at the season of Rosh Hashanah and Yom Kippur where the Jews get right with those they have sinned against). But we don't know *when* the Temple will be built. That's exactly like the Lord. God doesn't want us to worry about when the Temple will begin to be built. The aim for the 144,000 Jewish believers will be to preach to an unbelieving world. One needs to know that he will stop them from sacrificing.

The sacrificing is crucial because it begins the process of transformation from a conqueror of the world to a ruler of the entire people requiring their worship. He will hijack the worship of the Jews, which ends the time of peace for Israel.

Abomination of Desolation then Destruction of the Anti-Christ

Most struggle to comprehend the nature of why the Anti-Christ even cares about a tiny nation that doesn't have the military might of the Russians, Chinese or Americans. Why would he actually wish to harm these people? Here is why the Bible has been proven true again and again. He hates anything of God's.

Abomination means the grossest things that a person can do within the Temple. Consider every disgusting deed. Today, we are faced with the Adrenochrome (killing of children only after scaring them to their death and withdrawing the blood as collagen and injecting into their pores – as Sandra Bullock explained to Ellen DeGeneres on her show years ago) and the pillaging of children worldwide. It is assumed, by investigators, that Richard Branson caters to the royalty of the world, while the deceased Jeffery Epstein accomplished his dastardly deed of sex slavery on children, with celebrities, government officials and CEOs of industry in islands that were very close to one another in the Atlantic. Considering the disgusting nature of the wanton brutality for their own means of the Cabal, is it so hard to imagine that the Anti-Christ would begin that same practice upon the people of the world in the Temple?

Also, inside of this backdrop of this point of the Tribulation, which is indicated as the midpoint, we know that the Anti-Christ (Revelation 13) will be killed and raise from the dead in an faux resurrection, just like Jesus. Firstly, the Anti-Christ is a man who begins the Tribulation with the First Beast inside of him. When that First Beast comes on the planet in the past of Daniel's recollections, thousands or millions die. Therefore, the beginning of the Tribulation has this level of brutality. But once he is assassinated in the middle portion, we see that Satan comes into the Anti-Christ.

Satan has spent millennia accusing the Saints of God in Heaven, as noted in Job. He has access to the throne room of God, while he also wanders to and fro about the world seeking to kill, steal and destroys, of which he does to Job. But once the Temple in Heaven is closed to Angels and then Satan himself, he is cast down to the earth with great wrath "knowing his time is short" as Revelation 12:12 indicates about the nature of Satan. Satan is the enemy of the planet who wishes for domination of the hearts of men and women to worship after they receive the Mark of the Beast, indicated in Chapter 13.

But this disgusting Abomination culminates a Desolation for the Temple. That means that a place of life becomes incapable of life anymore. Satan will desecrate that which the Jews have worshiped. I think it's oddly fascinating that God allows the Jews to worship for a time in the Tribulation then shows their worship with the ancient rituals to be ineffectual, as Paul portrays so perfectly in the Book of Romans.

At the end of the conversation from Daniel 9:27, Daniel is told that the destruction of the Man of Lawlessness is separated for disposal. In Revelation 19-20, we note that Michael, the Archangel who shows up for Daniel to war for him and does so on other occasions, stands before Jesus in those last days (I would put that at the end of the Tribulation after Jesus has stepped upon the planet) and gathers his prey. Realize that Jesus doesn't fight evil. The Anti-Christ, the First Beast, the Second Beast who enters the False Prophet, and the soul with the spirit of Satan are bundled up by the powerful Michael to be placed in the Abyss for 1000 years until near the end of the Tribulation. At that time, Satan will be released once more to deceive the nations again for a time. But he is quashed, along with those who have rebelled against God, and he is removed from humanity forever to go into the Lake of Fire.

69

CHAPTER EIGHT

SPECIFIC COMPONENTS OF THE MARK

There are several critical components of the Mark of the Beast. As I have already mentioned, we need a few things in place before that can happen, namely, the Bride of Christ must be gone. She is holding back this evil. You might argue that the Church isn't in good shape and doesn't believe yet. You might also contend that she must be purified before her Master comes for her. That's the one I would love to answer most!

How does one purify what is already pure? But you are going to indicate that you sinned just yesterday and me today, right? But the difference is that Jesus paid the penalty of sin "from the foundation of the earth." He wasn't feeling that maybe you should do something to "attain" that forgiveness by being better. You took the bath of faith when you came to Jesus. Now, if you walked away willfully as I did late in high school to early college, then that's another thing.

I was too interested in girls later in high school and began to lose my "first love" as Revelation 2 chides the churches. Only at the beginning of college did I meet a beautiful girl that I fell for. I wrote her a song only to realize that it was unrequited puppy love. She dragged many young men back to the Lord through a gentle but firm hand, reminding them of their deparivity of sin in which they were wallowing. Too many mistook her attention as a prelude to a romantic relationship however. But she never gave any indication that that was her aim or even worked to lead me on. I guess if I spent some time, I would remember her name, but since I am happily married, I will just recall her in the line of Heaven, as I enter the gates to give her a big hug for what she did in my life.

Other than the willful walking away from God, as the Goats I believe do (see my new book on *The Sheep: the Bride I always wanted to Marry* on my website), the rest of us have lived with the lie of Satan who has told us that our sin is so bad that Jesus would have deigned to climb upon the Cross for me. The reality is that He paid the whole price for sin, which is why you must spend time within the Book of Romans to understand what He genuinely did for you.

I recommend the Believers who come to my class to answer back to Satan the following retort the next time he accuses you before the throne: "I am the Bride of Christ." Nothing more. What you will find is a fascinating reaction is that Satan can't respond that that is untrue. If Jesus said that about you (Ephesians 5), then it *must* be true. If your wife or husband does some stupid stuff in your life, do you delete him from your life? You just might if it were that bad because you wouldn't want to be married to him or her. But Jesus has seen all the stupid you could ever do or ever have done and still would repeat the process of His death. He does, on a daily basis, in our hearts, as we choose to die for Him so that He can accomplish the tremendous work for the Gospel. So, now that we know that Jesus will absolutely come back for me, what does the world have to look forward to?

The Changemaker

The critical verse that most rightfully quote when considering the Mark of the Beast is Revelation 13:18. "Here is wisdom: The one who has understanding must calculate the number of the Beast, because it is the number of a man. His number is 666." And while that is the basis of the Mark of the Beast, we need to know what drives this identifier of the Mark.

In verse 11 of the same chapter, another Beast comes up out of the earth having "two horns of like a lamb, but he sounded like a dragon." This is no one other than the infamous False Prophet who is the second beast after the Anti-Christ. Here is the uniqueness of the Second Beast or the False Prophet. He is like a lamb which is an oblique reference to Jesus, meaning that he may be a pastor or teacher from Christianity. But his words will resemble that of Satan. If you didn't know any better, you would think that his words are tinged with the truth of the Bible. You must understand the Word of God to realize that Satan is speaking lies.

Secondly, he "exercises all the authority of

the first beast on his behalf and compels the earth and those who live on it to worship the first beast, whose fatal wound was healed (vs. 12)." Here, the False Prophet initiates his agenda to require the people of the planet to worship the Beast (Anti-Christ) who has a fatal wound that is healed. It is generally believed that the Anti-Christ will be wounded around about the middle of the Tribulation and then be resurrected by Satan, who has fallen from Heaven, as he was kicked out of the throne room.

The desire of Satan, through his muse of the Anti-Christ, is the worship of the people, which is why he leaves Heaven before time started (Ezekiel 14 and Isaiah 28). The Devil wants to be like God and have humanity bow at his behest. The False Prophet's job is to create the vehicle of that changeover of the world.

False Prophet's Signs of Deception

This former pastor, inside of the False Prophet, who is named by the leader of the planet, will have the most impressive supernatural power anyone has seen that will rival any that superheroes could ever dream. The word Sign, in Greek, is *Semeion* which means a Mark or Token. Inside of the power of this future man, he will be able to miraculously place the Mark of the Beast upon the person without touching that individual, but then requiring him or her to worship the king of this present darkness. He can go as far as calling fire from the first heavens (this is not the

Heaven), but in our mind's eye, the atmosphere to create pyrotechnics that defies the imagination.

His whole job is to overwhelm the intellect of the people of the planet by placing the Mark of the Beast on them. But verse 14 takes it one step further: "He deceives those who live on the earth because of the signs that he is permitted to perform on behalf of the beast, telling those who live on the earth to make an image of the beast who had the sword wound and yet lived."

Verse 15 indicates that a spirit enters the image, so that those who don't worship right then and there their master of this earth, they will be killed. That sounds hauntingly similar to the Martyrs who will come later in the Tribulation who will die and present their case in front of the whole planet, helping people to make the right decision not to follow the Beast.

Verse 16 intimates that no one is immune from the Mark. Everyone will be required to receive this etching on his right hand or forehead. In 17, we find that no one can buy or sell.

Buying and Selling with the Mark

Most of us, when we consider this statement that no one can buy or sell without the Mark, intuitively know about the idea of not being able to purchase the essentials of living. But we forget about the businesses who will not be able to ply their wares without this transactional ability. It is so incomprehensible that the Bible was creating a Fiat currency before there was one and a digital one at that.

The Fiat currency does not allow for the buying and selling with real purchasing power that existed for thousands of years and was easily recognizable to traders of different lands with precious metals. The world will have an individual identifier for that purpose (Still don't believe that the Bible's already future seeking and knows what it couldn't have known in 95 AD with John writing this from Heaven?).

Many do not realize the impact upon the businesses that will be forced to accept this ugly system of oversight that will come relating to selling. They will have no choice. But consider how a company in the Tribulation will be forced to continue to operate.

Firstly, the Church is gone. Poof, seven hundred million (long story how I might get that statistic, but it's a massive number of hundreds of millions) of people will suddenly disappear. Workers, vendors, bankers, and customers are all gone in an instant. Business might trickle in and most won't be able to survive during this kind of panic backdrop. But if you have one of those mid-sized company who comes to Christ during the Tribulation, as many people will, they will then be required to submit to the restrictive standards of the Anti-Christ and his world system that runs roughshod over his business. No matter how much he might wish not to use the system, the business owner will be faced with a very extreme choice: close the practice/business or choose for the Mark, meaning that he will have to submit to one on himself. Daunting choice! But there will also be those who are unaware of the choice beforehand who finally must give in out of fear. They will be informed before they receive this life-altering choice that they must worship the Anti-Christ.

For the customer, she has noticed that she will have fewer options to choose for the necessities she once had. Governmental assistance will be a joke since so many would have been brought to destitution with the massive disappearances that she has noticed. What does she do? If she is convinced that this Anti-Christ character is the savior of the world, she will gladly place her hand out to chip her right hand, and swear an oath to the king of the world so that she may finally receive that assistance.

I had an employee who was with me for almost four years. She was quite good in certain aspects of her job for a time but was terribly fearful. We all tried to make a difference in her life, but she would cry at the drop of a hat if once ounce of change came at her doorstep. Knowing that we were moving to a new office and how she was not handling any of the changes well, I watched my son (an IT guy in college) set up her computer with a new printer/scanner combo. She was terrified by the newfangled system wanting to keep the antiquated dual device (printer and scanner) in working order even though the printer was dead. He spent forty-five minutes explaining how to scan and print with the new system very patiently. As I rescued him from the clutches of her fear, he casually threw over his shoulder that he would be happy to take away the old scanner. She bowed up and broke into tears that she couldn't do her job if he did so.

Reluctantly, with her fear and then anger burgeoning as well as knowing we would change everything at the new location, we had to let her go. I gently gave her all the information about Jesus, but she flatly rejected Him out of hand. I can, so sadly, say that she may put her hand out of the Image of the Beast knowing full well that her life was on the line if she didn't do that so that she could justify her way of living in her current state. The totality of the buying and selling will be complete.

But you must realize the genius of the Bible. How in the world did John in Revelation, who gave a type of currency, always with significant value such as Gold or other precious metals, know how to write a brilliant system that wouldn't exist until the 21st Century? You guessed it; he didn't! Only the Holy Spirit was able to see into our future to our present technology to accomplish a work of a digital currency that an identifier on the hand or forehead could procure the goods and services one would need.

Possible Implementation of the Mark

One thing that I can nearly guarantee is that most of us will be wrong about the implementation of the Mark of the Beast. Isn't that why you bought this book so that I could tell you? Uh…If I reported to you in 2018 that the world economy would grind to a halt right after the President was impeached but acquitted by the Senate from a virus, and the world would not die in droves (such as with a 10% mortality rate), you would have called me crazy! But wait, did I tell you that riots would break out over multiple cities and mayors would tell the police to allow the towns to burn? Oh, I forgot, businesses and people would be shamed for not wearing their masks in all places. On second thought, most of them should just stay closed if the Left had their way. You could protest arm in arm, but you can't go to church where you could spread the virus. Are you sick, man?

If we could not predict the cataclysmic events of 2020 as well as the global currency reset and its upheaval, how in the world am I going to display the exact events of the following:

1. Seven hundred million disappear from the planet, leaving grieving citizens and wrecks everywhere.
2. A massive peace treaty is signed with a leader who seems to get the people, along with his religious cohorts, working against the population of people trying to kill them.
3. War all over the planet breaks out in a limited nuclear engagement as well as troops toppling nations within days of the tactical nukes dropping.
4. Diseases worse than anyone could imagine leak from the deepest Biosafety Level 4 facilities to infect the world at 15% mortality rates not rivaled since the Spanish Flu of 1918.
5. Violence and looting continue with

complete anarchy inching from town to town as police and other government officials have died, left their posts, or were missing in the incredible disappearances.

These events would shape the way one considers their daily bread. It's possible that no one would go to work anymore, realizing that their jobs were not essential. They would be conjuring new ways to keep their family alive. Once the system begins to disintegrate, not to mention the rules of law, the social norms of politeness fly out the door along with those consecrations of compassionate interactions. That's when the survival instinct of men and women of all nations and races would kick into new levels of wanton destruction, deleting the rule of law.

Under the backdrop, one might be a shell of herself in the visage of the mirror three and a half years from the introduction of this world leader that has reigned over the chaos befallen humanity. It's possible that a hack could wreck one's credit, which therefore allows the person to submit to a local agency for the Mark of the Beast. The hack might push right passed the moral filters aligned in the chest of the individual to innervate Maslow's Hierarchy of essential needs to cloth and feed oneself. Bowing to the will of the government might suddenly seem as reasonable as getting the next iPhone upgrade did to them a few years earlier.

But I think that the Image of the Beast is a potential gamechanger for the False Prophet. No longer would you have these massive lines for only a few people devoted to inquiring for the requisite levels of compliance of worship, nope the program would ensure that. The Artificial Intelligence (AI) would run in the background as a nursing professional injected the needle as the parishioner would step into the next booth and talk to the Anti-Christ herself as she fulfilled the duties of her oath and continued existence upon the planet.

81

CHAPTER NINE

Is NESARA the Mark of the Beast?

One of the most extensive questions I have been asked since my YouTube channel made monetization was when I created my first video on NESARA. I have three great passions in my ministry with which to teach: 1) Hope in the Last Days (an End Time Teaching), 2) NESARA/GESARA and Money, and 3) Truth and Lies of What We Believe. The first was the last one on this list that I created. I love to teach people that the Bible can be proven correct in six verses of John 19:31-37 inside of Jesus' death (you can read that in "Our Secret Zombie Life"). I also deal with Predestination versus Free Will and topics of Evil that no one wants to discuss.

The Hope in the Last Days series always takes its toll when I teach it. It's a bit complicated but so helpful to the Body of Christ, since she has heard very little about the full compilation of the Word of God with End Time Teaching. Lastly, I love to research many topics about the Deep State in all the ways that these nefarious governmental agencies have defrauded America and the world. The wanton destruction of cultures and people, not to mention the killing of little children (as I write this in August of

2020, you may or may not have had your eyes opened upon the topic of child sacrifices by the Cabal for their own pleasure), leads to me to share on the topic of money. Why money? Why not the children? Money is the "root of all types of evil!" Isn't money bad?

Some people want to bring to the surface an ill that they see within our society; police brutality that requires some re-education of our officers who mostly protect us. Of course, we will pick out the bad seeds which are abhorrent when it is done so under the guise of authority with a gun. But the systemic issues are much more profound than anyone believes. It goes to the cash endemic inside our system. Nathan Rothschilds intimated that he didn't care who ran the government if he was able to manage the flow of the money.

The question on most commenters' minds: isn't NESARA/GESARA another type of control that brings about the Mark of the Beast? As you have already read so far, we must have the Beast before you can perceive the aim of what the Anti-Christ wishes to do. Let me detail a little more of what it means significantly after the massive majority of those who will take the Mark will notice.

This Present Time and the Mark

Will and Chris (wonderful teachers and friends of mine) have been working with two new types of teachings: one is the seven spirits of God (actually the personalities of God and how they interact in one's life), and second is the twelve dynamics of God. Both are interactive with one another. They are personalities and abilities of God in how He interacts with His creation as well as how humanity can flow with the creator.

One of the dynamics I have understood so clearly is called *This Present Time*. In Genesis, God created all things. In Revelation 13:8, John states that "before the foundation of the world, the Lamb was slain." Therefore, before time began, He had created a way for humanity to interact with His creation. It was done before the earth started but had to have a time in which that reality intersected with Time on the planet.

In Revelation 9:15, it records, "So the four angels who were prepared for the hour, day, month and year were released to kill a third of the human race." Without detailing this dreadful portion of the last world war of humankind that I believe occurs approximately 13 months before the end of the Tribulation, this Scripture has captured my heart for many years. The Lord conceives that an exact moment in time is set for something to occur by eternal standards. At "that" Present Time, one of the most major wars in human history will be waged, and God already knew it to happen for that moment.

Therefore, when we apply that logic of God knowing the future, He has set a plan in motion for the Mark of the Beast to occur as well as a plan for the NESARA timing of release to occur before the Mark. Satan would love for nothing more than to unleash his dreams he has had from time immemorial to enslave the human race, but God is saying that He has a different plan. Doesn't that excite you that the God of the Universe has this in control?

MARTYRS FOR GOD

Fast forward with me a few years into a future and embedded deep within the Tribulation to find a moment in which the Mark has been widely disseminated. It could easily have its peak of usage within a few months with lengthy lines for a quick and simple process of receiving your Mark, registering your identity with the chip implanted, and then worshipping your new earthly deity. There will be Believers in Christ that the Bible calls the Saints of God (I use another reference of the Kaleo or Called) who will come forward once the traitors point them out to humanity for their non-compliance with the worldwide law. They will suffer greatly at the hands of the False Prophet and who I also believe are the Goat Teachers who follow the False Prophet in propagating the information of obedience.

The Saints of God will give their life up as a sacrifice pleasing to the One who made them in holy defiance to the powers of this spiritual darkness. They will be able to help, by their ultimate sacrifice and that insubordination, those who have *not* received the Mark of the Beast. Remember, we have to have the Remnant of God (the last third of the Jewish people who will come to Jesus at the last Rosh Hashanah) and the Sheep Nations who will view God in the clouds and come to Him with hearts renewed into the Millennial Reign of Christ. Will the Saints do that galvanizing these people against getting the Mark of the Beast but not really giving in to the call of God? I absolutely believe so!

What Does NESARA/GESARA Do?

On my YouTube channel, some guy decided to drop his website, asking me what I thought. I clicked on his site to find that NESARA was of the Devil just as it would bring about the Mark of the Beast. This is a tremendously common theme among Christians in late August of 2020. By the time you are reading my book, you may already know truths that I am revealing now, but I will detail them for you.

GESARA/NESARA
1. *National Monies (countries come with their own backed currencies)*
2. *Increase of freedom for the common people due to Constitutional (or Common Law) practices in the nations*
3. *No Global or individual worship required. If you hate Trump now, you are allowed to do so while you still receive the benefits of the systems in place for NESARA/GESARA*
4. *Reversing of National Debt, Personal Debt and Corporate Debt*
5. *Hard currency creates stability that creates less artificial control of any agency*
6. *Becomes a performance-based system of worth (we will explain)*

> *7. True humanitarian efforts worldwide without the nefarious nature of the 501(c)(3) governmental standards*

Now, on the surface, does this resemble an atheistic standard of reducing one's freedoms? Do we see a requirement of worshipping the one who brings the currency? Do we see the nature of the laws that are pragmatic (everchanging to the whims of the Elite)? Nope!

Donald Trump comes to the table with the NESARA/GESARA concept that will inevitably be called something different (although it may stay the same for which is something I would wish). NESARA brings America back to the Constitutional Law that was created by our Founding Fathers, while GESARA is the interaction of the world within the American Framework of NESARA. The Founding Fathers were, in many cases, Freemasons who are nefarious due to their globalist ideals, but those concepts were not found inside of the Constitution or the Articles of Confederation. The Constitution was a Law system based upon morality unearthed within the Biblical standards created thousands of years earlier instead of the ever-changing laws that spurn justice for inequality for one's acts in a Republic. The lawyers and judges will have to be retrained in Constitutional Law and cannot be holding people based upon the whims of the Attorney-Client Privilege that doesn't protect the people but criminals.

Once people note that the national debt of $26.6 (in August of 2020) is completely wiped out, the need for the Internal Revenue Service (IRS) has no need to collect wages. Titus 5:18, "For the Scripture says: Do not muzzle an ox while it is treading out the grain, and the worker is worthy of his wages." The muzzling is the implementation reducing the efforts of the worker and the business to function at full capacity while the wages being taken is seen as an unrighteous act against the person by a government.

Of course, there would have to be taxation, but the creators of the NESARA plan knew that without the corruption and waste of government, a sales tax of 14% or so could be taken for only non-essential items (nothing for groceries, medicines and resale items to name a few). That pittance of the sales has always been known as a *Fair Tax* standard in that those who are purchasing more luxury items above their basic needs are paying a higher tax for those items. It's ultimately fair for those who earn more versus those who are on the lower end of the wage scale.

A performance-based rewards system would entail that those who are producing capital would benefit from their labors even more. At this time, we have senators who do so truly little for $174K a year and receive that for the rest of their lives as well as massive incentives of health care you and I would never see. Many of them also come out of the Congress and Senate with millions in their pocket toward their pet projects of lobbyists who gold plate their hands. Whereas the people who create real value of the economy, such as workers and real public servants, earn much less. Wouldn't you rather see a police officer make $174K a year to reduce the potential of corruption with significant oversite inside of his or her job than a Senator?

Some of the 501C3 organizations that are tax-exempt, outside of churches, are skirting the law, such as the Clinton Foundations and others stating their supposed good works but bilking the public for all they are worth. Haiti's devastating earthquake in 2010 brought in billions to that nation that never fell to the people with one of the vehicles for that money being the Clinton Foundation. Don't walk into Haiti with the title of the Clinton Foundation on your breast pocket if you don't want to be attacked for your thievery! Those billions came right into the foundation with no benefit to the people.

On the other hand, many churches set up this legal vehicle to benefit humanity for their charitable works of homeless and poor populations of different types of classes. But churches and other legitimate foundations feel the burden of proof on them to tow the governmental lines while the illegitimate as listed above and many others that entail ill-gotten booty go unpunished.

Once the money of a country, based upon their own points of wealth, line up underneath as a basis for their currency is calculated, some of the poorest countries in the world who have been decimated by the world system of Fiat and Intelligence organizations of the world trying to control the wealth under the feet of the people (diamonds, gold and precious metals in South

America, Africa and Asia).   That release of currency toward their own country's needs increases the standard of living for the people that thereby allows the people to purchase more again, expanding the wealth of the world. Those that believe that there is a finite amount of wealth of the world believe this is based on the fraudulent concepts that the Cabal has spilled through the media. Their lies enslave the people of the world upon the worthless Fiat monetary system that none of us have lived without.

How does the Mark differ from NESARA?

Mark of the Beast Currency
1. *Global money based on Fiat (worthless standard)*
2. *Reduction of liberties given to a select few with billions in capital*
3. *Eventual worship of one man under the monetary system*
4. *Promotion of one-world government.*
5. *Promotion of one currency (no national currency)*
6. *Promotes atheistic means of religion into worship of one man (Anti-Christ)*
7. *World system creates poorer culture of people requiring the government's support for their basic needs creating a sheep mentality to bend to their will*
8. *Pragmatic Law based on what the Elite wishes for the world to enact that would be clouded in their lies*

I am going to skip around these above areas a bit since some of them have already been addressed effectively in other chapters. But the aim of the Central Bankers of the globe was to create a One World government, currency and religion. From Woodrow Wilson's 13 points of global response in 1918 to a body of nations that would clog the affairs of the world by a global elite, all were created artificially. The English and French wanted Germany to pay and they had no choice. But that level of the bankruptcy of Germany created inflation that was off the chart. By 1933, a loaf of bread would cost about one billion Reich Marcs. They would paper the walls with the Fiat currency that had no value. This level of criminal devaluing of the currency spread to America, as I talked about in earlier chapters, to enslave the world under its auspices.

Therefore, the world government was formed until Japan showed that it had no teeth to enforce anything as they backed out of the treaty to kill vast portions of China in the mid-1930s. After World War Two and with the death of the League of Nations, America, along with her new allies of France, England, the Soviet Union and others, formed the United Nations whose main goal was the spreading of globalism.

They became a police force and created a coalition of nations to quell a communist uprising in North Korea, in which two million died during 1950-1953. In that war, the world found a new way to interact under the periscope of the Elite who formed our opinions of what they wished to do. That led to the CIA to invade and enslave nation after nation inside of its anti-red propaganda. Further stated, the CIA spread their global agenda under the guise that they would rebuild that third world country after America, inside of the clandestine CIA forces, could rape the people of the land their goods. American companies were allowed to enrich the Cabal and themselves, which created a worldwide stranglehold upon the money supply. That's their Modus Operandi. They wish for their word to be final upon what they steal and what they do as law. Don't get in their way without severe repercussions to your business, life and security.

Inside of this quick synopsis, of which you may have never heard the official story, we see the nature of the pragmatic rule of law that is everchanging against the wishes and the needs of the people of country after country including America. We look like the bad guy, but in reality, we haven't done the evil that they wrought. It is the Cabal. And that's precisely in line with the Mark of the Beast.

Personal Story of Liberty with Money

As I have already shown, the history of the Federal Reserve as well the Central Bankers of the world have done a number on the Fiat currency that has no value outside of what they state it has. Inflation is a weapon against the people with which we don't have any defense. Doesn't that sound like a lack of freedom to do what you will? Let me talk a little about freedom within this financial system that will ultimately help you in the next monetary revaluation.

In 2008, I was 425K in debt with the biz. I had no way out. I had been a Bible study leader and studied the Scriptures for most of my life, but realized I had only scratched the surface of complexity with the Lord. I dug into my circumstance with the Lord. Instead of a hundred-foot depth with God, I was suddenly sinking my submarine to seven hundred foot depths with the Holy Spirit. You might find this silly to focus on God when my business was flushing down the toilet. Some did tell me precisely who only had a passing knowledge of what was happening in my life. If I did declare bankruptcy from a professional level since I also had Personal Guarantee loans of a unique structure, it would have dripped right over into Foreclosure and Personal Bankruptcy to boot. It wasn't an easy time.

From 2010 to 2011, I would ask the Lord if I should declare bankruptcy from month to month with the finances so bad that I could barely pay anyone and seemed to sink deeper into debt, but in reality, I was coming out of it. After six months of those questions, the Lord told me to "Shut up! Don't you know that I know it would take four to six months to offload your files of the practice to another Audiologist who could take care of the patients? I never want you to ask me that again!"

This monologue with God startled me into silence but a little more confusion until I fleshed it out a bit more. He didn't say I would or would not need to declare bankruptcy, but that He didn't want to hear about it. I stopped asking the question and began to trust. At the same time, I was digging into the Word with my friend Will who was teaching me the Liberty of God's personality inside of money. I learned that true liberty only comes with trust in the One who made us and has already seen all that we will ever know.

I began to employ a process that another friend of mine used. James would put all his bills in a basket. He knew every dollar that was supposed to come in and all that was outgoing. He would only pay that bill once the Lord told him to do so. At that point, I was skeptical but listening since Will was explaining the same thing. These two men of God weren't blown by the winds of obligation that the financial system created inside of the debtor; they were flowing inside of the River of God, and His wisdom for how He would handle the money situation.

I put every bill in front of the Lord with full knowledge of the incoming and outgoing bills for a larger practice in the Tulsa area. But the larger it is, the more I need to feed the seven employees I have now in 2020. I also realized that God has seen how He wants me to pay vendors. Sometimes, He has required the government to pay me back (long story of miracles with audits), and how he wanted the vendors to interact with me. It's not all on me. It's on the One who created me. But that deep dive into the Word netted me another phrase that the Lord uttered: "If you pay attention to the things that are important to me, I will pay attention to the things that are important to you." I live by that God axiom daily.

95

CHAPTER TEN

Global Money vs. National Money inside of God

The next question to address inside of our discussion is this: if we are swinging back to more freedom in this NESARA reset, doesn't the Mark go away then? Yes, for a time. No, in due time. God is intervening in a way that we haven't experienced because of the evil that exists. That's true. But, it does not mean that the Bible is proven wrong and the prophecies about Jesus' return are false! It's simply not time for God to initiate His plan.

Throughout our national history, we have seen moments in time in which the currency was controlled by the national agencies. It is exactly what Abraham Lincoln was killed for in his second term after the Civil War had concluded. It was one of the mysteries of the 1800s about how a president who survived the great conflict but was killed after its conclusion. Lincoln had initiated a Green Back Dollar which swung away from the Central Banking system to a national currency. John F. Kennedy wanted the Gold-Backed Dollar back in force as well as to "break the CIA into a thousand pieces" in his famous speech in 1963. Both great presidents were fighting for the renewal of a swing to national currency to defund the fraud perpetrated on the people of America. Both were killed inauspicious and conspiratorial means that have yet to be fully uncovered.

Donald Trump is aware of the sins of the past on both sides of the currency fence. He knows how JFK was killed and why. He has been formulating a plan to wrest control away from the evil bankers who sacrifice children for their own longevity of life (see Adrenochrome and PizzaGate scandals as the tip of the iceberg). There will be a time of peace when nations finally realize that they weren't fighting against one another but were pawns in a chess match. The Global Bankers threw them under the bus of tyranny to further their profits in the wake of global conflicts of the numerous wars of the 20th century and beyond.

Matt Moore, Crypto Moore YouTube Channel, is a friend of mine in the Tulsa area. I have spoken at his group called Young Businessmen of Tulsa twice. After the most recent time in which I detailed my own healing walking out of a hospital in three days without any side effects (you can see my whole story on my YouTube channel too), Matt wanted to do a series on NESARA and then NESARA with End Time connotations. We discussed the gate that winds from globalism inside of the Fiat currency back to a Nationalism inside of the currency backed by precious metals.

The Word of God clearly states that there *will* be a One World Leader that will be privately referred to as the Anti-Christ, who will rise after the Bride of Christ has disappeared from the planet. This leader will be imbued by the power of a Beast that has always caused chaos and death when it enters the realm of humanity because he is a spirit that hates us. He will then promote a False Prophet with his own spirit, called the Second Beast to create the vehicle of worship. The False Prophet will set up the One World Currency and the One World Religion that the Cabal has longed for a long time.

Bill Clinton, Barack Obama, George W. Bush and Bush, Sr, were all part of the Cabal to defraud humanity out of their money and lives to create the world's most incredible messes. Those criminal debacles include George Herbert Walker Bush being in Dallas on November 22, 1963, by the then FBI Director's notation of his complicity in the JFK planning to assassinate a sitting president along with the FBI, CIA, Dallas Police and the Secret Service in the continued coverup.

Clinton and his wife had dozens of people killed in the wake of their own satanic scandals and pedophilia in defrauding America from its money and innocence. George W. Bush was intimately involved in the planning and execution of September 11th, 2001, in the killing of 3000 people and the wars of Iraq and Afghanistan with countless lives all to feed their thirst for globalism. Obama has guided the planet toward his brand of globalism in blocking the entry of the Gold-Back currency, as did Bush Junior in his time in the White House.

Democrat and Republican alike a complicit in these significant crimes. And that's why it took someone outside of the political swamp to drain it of its filth with Donald Trump.

That all said only leads to the next point after the Revaluation of the Currency occurs in 2020 and 2021. There will be a fundamental way that we consider our finances. We will need to learn a new set of norms, not the lies the media tells you about the norms of ridiculous social distancing and masks daily. We will find that debt is *not* our friend. When the debt is released from each person on the planet (yes it will!), it's not going to be a license to purchase so much that you become a statistic on the roadmap to crime and bankruptcy to feed your new habit. You will need sound money advice and a steep learning curve.

I mentioned at the beginning of this book that Americans, as well as the world, will have to stop perceiving money as the devil or boring. They will have to understand that currency is only a vehicle to your goals. Once people are allowed to consider their dreams, it will unlock a portion of freedom where we can think outside of ourselves for a time to benefit the world around us. Those who have more will be able to give even more. Those who have a little will be able to give a bit more.

Jesus gave many references to this type of sacrificial giving in the Widow's Mite when a pharisee chose to elevate himself high for his gigantic tithe where the poor widow gave a mite, which is less than a penny. Jesus intimated that her percentage was higher in currency and in the spirit. The parable of the Talents will also become a point of wisdom that all must investigate (I do so on my YouTube channel a little more).

How Will it Swing Back?

If we know that the Bible will be fulfilled and it has been true all along, then how can we fundamentally believe that the nature of the world in its unceasing change affects the eternal God? Hebrews 13:8 states, "Jesus Christ is the same yesterday, today, and forever." So, He is ever *Unchanging*; therefore, He will accomplish His plans for a Tribulation and a Mark of the Beast once he is introduced by the King of kings in Revelation 6 when the First Seal is opened.

Few, unfortunately, quote the next verse: "Don't be led astray by various kinds of strange teachings; for it is good for the heart to be established by grace and not by goods since those in them have not benefited." While Paul was speaking of sacrificial foods that were banned by the Jews and the new Hebrew Christians were struggling with their past beliefs from the Old Testament to the New Testament, Paul was making a profound comment toward being led astray by strange teachings.

To be "led astray" means to be removed or taken away from a particular path. Add that to "strange teachings" is a fascinating word that English loves to steal to explain itself: *Xenos Didache. Xenos* is where we derive xenobiology which is alien to our own or also separated without knowledge of the other. *Didache* is the doctrine that one might believe outside of the Word of God. Therefore, we have a marriage of alien teachings that are doctrines outside of the Truth that the Word gives us. I am seeing this today in so many ways when we apply this new knowledge of NESARA versus the Mark of the Beast. NESARA is not wrong whatsoever. Money is just a vehicle not to be worshiped or elevated by what it can do as an exchange of goods and services. That's IT!

But for those to teach that the Mark of the Beast is the NESARA, you are missing the point of what Donald Trump and his cadre of believers are trying to generate - freedom from debt that the Bible refers to as a Debt Jubilee. In the Old Testament, a Debt Jubilee was to be afforded to the people every seven years.

Most of the debt that the ancient person accumulated was owed to the king of the land. If the burden were too great, the debt would stunt his economy for the future into complete stagnation. So, it was therefore not as magnanimous as one might imagine for a king to do so even though it could curry public favor for his policies and create a more friendly environment for the growth of his kingdom. But the Debt Forgiveness that is to come releases the shackles of the unrighteous debt that the Cabal has placed around the necks of the world in which they *did not* participate in creating. Only the Cabal did it!

After a time of peacefulness, there will be a swing back to a debt economy in which the world will require security based upon an external threat. Typically, to get a population of people to relinquish their freedoms, fear and propaganda must proliferate enough to create a push to protect the citizens. It normally comes within the auspices of war or an unseen enemy such as pandemics. The Cabal in 2020 have tried to accomplish that level of paranoia but to no avail in the long run. Fear will run its course and lead to anger at the one who isn't explaining truth. The Mainstream Media, which includes both sides of the political aisle, obfuscate through their pundits of opinion and emotion incite a "Cool Whip" lather in the American people to flow in the Cabal's direction. But once the Red Pill is swallowed whole by the general public, the gig is up for the Cabal, and they will find themselves in jail or worse for their crimes against humanity.

Peace almost never lasts on this planet. One side becomes exceedingly jealous of another and wishes to procure that booty for himself. When the smallest of provocations stirs into the mind of the corrupt leader, then I believe something like the Ezekiel 38-39 War will ensue. Russia's leader and her country, Gog and Magog, respectfully, will create a pact to incite war against Israel and be thwarted for their efforts. Then a peace treaty is needed to filter through the nations to protect the world from the emboldened Israelis who wish to punish the aggressors (as they always have in their recent past from 1948 to now) for their sins against her people.

Cheer up, friends. Luke 12:35-37 (by the way, that's one of my favorite chapters in the whole Bible) starts an End Time conversation in which Jesus comes to settle accounts with the people of the planet in a different fashion to when and who they align themselves with. God calls His Bride *Faithful.* "Be ready for service and have your lamps lit. You must be like people waiting for their master to return from the wedding banquet so that when He comes and knocks, they can open the door for Him at once. Those slaves the master will find alert when He comes will be blessed. I assure you: He will get read, have them recline at the table, then come and serve them." Then in verse 42, Jesus continues: "The Lord said: 'Who then is the faithful and sensible manager His master will put in charge of His household servants to give them their allotted food at the proper time?'"

Firstly, Jesus is discussing the Wedding and Wedding Feast. Who is the Bride? You are! Who is the Faithful? The one who waits for her husband to come for her. Again, you are! Who gives the servants of God their food at the allotted time? You do! It's not about food here, but an allegory the Groom wanting His Bride to know that she has the keys to the kingdom inside of the Bible and the food is what sustains the world.

During this time of NESARA freedoms, we will be about setting up the people of the world the vehicles that will bring about the Saints who learn about Christ during the Tribulation a way for them to survive the Tribulation on the other end of the equation to come into the Millennial Reign. But it will be a time that is hundreds of times worse in all scope to any time we have lived in before or since. Do the work that God has called you to!

REFERENCES

1. "105 Years Later: Did the Sinking of the Titanic lead to the Creation of the Federal Reserve?" The Pontiac Review, Joe Bowman, April 14. 2017, https://pontiactribune.com/2017/04/105-years-later-did-the-sinking-of-the-titanic-lead-to-the-creation-of-the-federal-reserve/
2. "The End: A Complete Overview of Bible Prophecy and the End of Days," Dr. Mark Hitchcock, August 1, 2012, Tyndale Publishing.
3. "The Killing of Uncle Sam: The Demise of the United States of America," Rodney Howard-Browne and Paul L. Williams, 2018, River Publishing, Tampa, FL.
4. "NESARA: The National Economic Stabilization and Recovery Act," 108th Congress, Second Session, NESARA.Org

OTHER WORK CONTRIBUTIONS

- "The World Global Settlement Funds," Alcuin and Flutterby, April 12, 2015, https://alcuinbramerton.blogspot.com/2010/10/world-global-settlement-funds.html
- Articles on Real History, https://www.realhistorychannel.org/covid-19:-a-military-plan-to-save-the-world
- Constitutional Law Reporter, November 12, 2019, Amendment 14: Section 4.

ABOUT THE AUTHOR

Dr. Scott Young, CCC-A, FAAA, an Audiologist since 1991, and owns Hearing Solution Centers, Inc. in Tulsa, OK. Besides World War II studies, his passions include writing, Sci-Fi and singing. He has written a fictional novel, *The Violin's Secret,* which chronicles the survival of one young teenager through the Holocaust. *Singing in the Mind: A Study of the Voice and Song* was his first non-fictional writing about the passion of singing and a different view of how singing occurs in the mind and its role in the culture.

Professor in History was his third, but second fictional book of a man who is an atheist but has the fantastic opportunity to ask Jesus unique questions on various topics. *ForeTold - Book 1 and 2* chronicles the End of the Earth from a Biblical perspective in a fictional form. There are other books fiction and non-fiction that may be of interest to you! More information can be found at www.DrScottYoung.com.

Dr. Young is a unique communicator in the way he perceives the world, as his wife, Wendy, and his son, Stefan, will attest. My thanks go to Wendy and Sue Reidel, who read this book quite thoroughly to find my errors.